# MUSHROOMS

# MUSHROOMS

A QUANTUM BOOK

Published by Grange Books
an imprint of Grange Books Plc
The Grange
Kingsnorth Industrial Estate
Hoo, nr. Rochester
Kent ME3 9ND

ISBN 1-84013-251-5

This book is produced by
Quantum Books Ltd
6 Blundell Street
London N7 9BH

Project Manager: Rebecca Kingsley
Project Editor: Judith Millidge
Design/Editorial: David Manson
Andy McColm, Maggie Manson

The material in this publication previously appeared in
*The Mushroom Identifier*

QUMSPMM
Set in Futura
Reproduced in Singapore by Eray Scan
Printed in Singapore by Star Standard Industries (Pte) Ltd

# Contents

# FASCINATING FUNGI

The Fungi kingdom is enormous. It is a group of living organisms which are quite distinct from either animals or plants, and the group is probably as large as, or larger than, either. There are probably more than 8000 species to be found growing in North America and Europe alone. Some are deliciously edible, while others are so deadly poisonous that even a small amount will kill.

# Major Fungi Groups

Fungi may be found in a great variety of forms. But in order to spread and multiply, all fungi produce spores and form special structures, called fruitbodies, which are specifically designed for this purpose.

## CLASSIFICATION

Fungi are classified according to the manner in which they produce spores and the type of fruitbody they develop. There are seen to be three main classes of fungi: the Zygomycetes, Ascomycetes and the Basidiomycetes.

## THE ZYGOMYCETES

The Zygomycetes are the thread-fungi and pin-moulds, and do not normally form a fruitbody which is sufficiently large to be seen by the naked eye. Being so small, they are discussed no further in this mainly photographic account.

*Left.* Polyporus squamosus – a bracket-fungi – shows there are many other types of fungi as well as the familiar mushrooms.

*Above.* Stropharia aeruginosa is a very distinctive, green, poisonous, woodland toadstool of the Basidiomycetes class.

## THE ASCOMYCETES

The Ascomycetes produce their spores (usually eight) within a single 'cell', called an ascus and their fruitbodies may be open cup- or disc-shaped structures when they are called Discomycetes or flask-shaped structures when they are known as Pyrenomycetes.

## THE BASIDIOMYCETES

The Basidiomycetes produce their spores (usually four) on short stalks known as sterigmata at the top of a club-shaped cell, called a basidium. The fruitbodies are the fungi with which readers will be most familiar of all – mushrooms, and toadstools.

# Collecting Wild Fungi

Fleshy fungi tend to appear seasonally. The most productive months are those of autumn, starting after the summer heat has passed and continuing through to the first frosts of early winter.

## WHEN TO COLLECT

As the autumn progresses, the collection of species growing on the ground may become difficult as fallen leaves can obscure fruit-bodies. The length of the season varies according to the climate. In the UK and the rest of Europe and on the Eastern Coast of North America there are two seasons, spring (April–May) and autumn (August–November). Because of the range of fruiting times in the rest of North America, it is not possible to be precise as to the season for individual species.

*Left.* Amanita phalloides, *the Death Cap, deadly poisonous even in small amounts.*

*Above.* Daldinia concentrica, *King Alfred's Cakes grows on dead or dying trees.*

## HOW TO COLLECT

Large fungi are easily collected because they lack any deeply penetrating root systems. Care must always be taken however not to damage the roots and branches of trees or to uproot neighbouring plants. Only collect good healthy specimens. Do not pick more fruitbodies than you really need, but ensure that you have sufficient specimens to show all the stages of development.

Picking must be done carefully as many species are brittle and it is easy to leave behind the base of the fruitbody which may be important when it comes to identification. A sharp knife is essential and a hand-trowel is useful. Plastic bags are to be avoided as the fruitbodies will 'sweat' and are easily squashed. Keeping the species separate is vital especially if collecting for the dinner table.

# Mushrooms and Toadstools

Mushrooms and toadstools form the bulk of the species illustrated in this book, and are the fungi which are most frequently observed. They are especially frequent in woodlands during the autumn months.

### MUSHROOMS & TOADSTOOLS

There is no scientific distinction between a mushroom and a toadstool, and there are also many exceptions to the common belief that 'mushrooms' are edible while toadstools are usually poisonous. Traditionally both terms exist in the English language, whereas only a single term exists in most other languages.

### AGARICALES ORDER

The scientific term for these fungi is agarics (order Agaricales). They are Basidiomycetes, producing their spores on gills, which radiate out from the underside of a cap that is usually although not always supported by a centrally attached stem, they are mostly soft fleshy fungi growing very quickly but surviving only a few days.

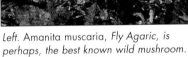

*Left.* Amanita muscaria, *Fly Agaric, is perhaps, the best known wild mushroom.*

*Above. There are more than 5000 species of mushroom in the northern hemisphere.*

## CLUES TO IDENTIFICATION

There are very many families of mushrooms and toadstools which are distinguished largely by the differences in their microscopic structures. One of the vital field characteristics which is used for identifying them is the colour of their spores when deposited in mass. Species may be white-, pink-, brown-, or black-spored. Other valuable identity clues include presence of the protective layers called veils and the way the gills are attached to the stem.

## DEADLY MUSHROOMS

Mushrooms and toadstools include the commercial, edible mushrooms, the deadly poisonous *Amanita* species, the brightly-coloured brittle gills, the milk-caps, oyster caps and wax gills.

**Remember.** Many mushrooms contain hallucinogenic poisons which can cause delirium and coma. Some are so poisonous that even small amounts can kill. <u>Take care and always wash your hands after mushroom picking.</u>

# Other Types of Fungi

Readers will be familiar with mushrooms and toadstools, but there are many other examples of 'larger fungi' such as bracket-fungi, club-fungi, tooth-fungi, puffballs, stinkhorns, jelly-fungi, cup-fungi and flask-fungi.

**CHANTERELLES** This group includes fleshy fungi with thick ridges and blunt edges. The Chanterelle is one of the best-known edible fungi served in restaurants.

**BOLETES** Mostly soft and fleshy, with a short life-span, the boletes are related to mushrooms. They are regarded as the most highly prized of the edible fungi.

**CLUB- AND TOOTH-FUNGI** Soft and fleshy, and often brightly coloured. Most are harmless but they are rarely recommended for eating as some can cause stomach upsets.

**BRACKET-FUNGI** A large group which grow on wood. They are the most advanced type of fungi with a tough protective crust to protect against the weather and insects.

*Left. Bracket-fungi have a tough texture and develop slowly, being long-lived.*

*Above. Oudemansiella radicata, Rooting Shank, grows on underground tree roots.*

**PUFFBALLS** This group has developed a fruitbody which remains unopened and encloses the spores. When young, the fruit-bodies are white, fleshy and edible.

**STINKHORNS** A soft 'egg-stage' with a membranous outer layer is initially formed. This eventually ruptures to release a tall spongy stem with a strong unpleasant smell.

**JELLY-FUNGI** Resembling a blob of jelly not easily recognised as fungi. These species are not really edible, however, some are found in Chinese cuisine, though they are used more for texture than flavour.

**CUP- AND FLASK-FUNGI** These fungi can grow on soil, other fungi, dung or on animal remains. Morels and truffles are examples which are regularly collected and eaten as delicacies.

## HABITATS

The larger fungi species are very much dependent on the habitat in which they live. For this reason the directory part of this book is divided into seven sections which relate to fungi habitats.

1. On the ground in woodlands;
2. On the ground in grasslands;
3. On trees, stumps or debris;
4. In bogs or marshlands;
5. On burnt ground or wood;
6. On dung or enriched soil;
7. On other fungi.

# MUSHROOMS & FUNGI

### Key to symbols

A number of icons are used throughout the directory to provide a snapshot of the idiosyncrasies of each species.

## SEASON

| Spring | Summer | Autumn | Winter |

## EDIBILITY

Edible     Inedible

## TOXICITY

Deadly poisonous     Highly poisonous

**WARNING!** Many mushrooms contain poisons which can cause delirium and coma. Some are so poisonous that even small amounts can kill. <u>Take care and always wash your hands after mushroom picking.</u>

## CANTHARELLUS CIBARIUS THE CHANTERELLE OR THE GIROLLE

A bright orange-yellow, fleshy mushroom with thick branching ridges descending down the stem instead of thin gills.

**Group** Chanterelles.
**Season** Summer to autumn.
**Edibility** Excellent, much sought after.
**Cap** 3–15cm (1$^1$/4–6in) diameter.
**Stem** Short and tapering and solid.
**Flesh** Thick, pale yellow, apricot odour.
**Spore deposit** White.
**Habitat** Under beech and oak.

## CANTHARELLUS TUBAEFORMIS AUTUMN CHANTERELLE

A coniferous woodland species, often found in great numbers, but may be difficult to see in the litter. Distinguishable by the scaly cap, greyish and forking gills, and the yellowish stem.

**Group** Chanterelles.
**Season** Autumn.
**Edibility** Good.
**Cap** 2–6cm (1$^3$/4–2in) diameter.
**Stem** Flattened and hollow.
**Flesh** Thin, but firm, pleasant smell.
**Spore deposit** White.
**Habitat** Among forest litter.

## LEPISTA SAENA BLEWIT

A large fleshy mushroom, similar to the Wood Blewit, but lacking liliaceous tints in the cap and stem.

**Group** Mushrooms and Toadstools.
**Season** Winter.
**Edibility** Excellent.
**Cap** 5–12cm (2–4$^1$/4in) diameter.
**Stem** Thick, mauve, fibrous-scaly.
**Flesh** Thick and firm, white colour.
**Spore deposit** Pale pinkish.
**Habitat** Among leaf litter.

## CLITOCYBE CLAVIPES CLUB-FOOTED CLITOCYBE

A white-spored species with decurrent gills, and a conspicuously swollen stem base.

**Group** Mushrooms and Toadstools.
**Season** Autumn.
**Edibility** Edible, but can produce allergic reactions. Avoid eating with alcohol.
**Cap** 3–8cm (1$^1$/4–3in) diameter.
**Stem** Swollen near base, greyish and spongy.
**Flesh** Thick and white.
**Spore deposit** White.
**Habitat** Under both deciduous trees and conifers.

## CLITOCYBE ODORA BLUE-GREEN CLITOCYBE

Distinguished by the bluish green cap, whitish gills, and the strong odour of anise.

**Group** Mushrooms and Toadstools.
**Season** Autumn.
**Edibility** Edible, can be dried for use as a condiment.
**Cap** 3–7cm (1 1/4–2 3/4in) diameter.
**Stem** Whitish or greenish, with a woolly base.
**Flesh** Thin, pale, with a strong odour.
**Spore deposit** White.
**Habitat** Woodland near oak.

## LYOPHYLLUM CONNATUM WHITE LYOPHYLLUM

Forming pure white clusters on rich, peaty soil, usually at the edge of paths and in woodland clearings. Care must be taken not to confuse this species with the poisonous white *Clitocybe* species.

**Group** Mushrooms and Toadstools.
**Season** Autumn.
**Edibility** Edible but must be boiled first.
**Cap** 3–10cm (1 1/4–4in) diameter.
**Stem** Cylindrical, white to greyish.
**Flesh** White, firm with an alkaline smell.
**Spore deposit** White.
**Habitat** Mixed woodland, can be in long rows.

## TRICHOLOMA SULPHUREUM  SULPHUR TRICHOLOMA

A uniformly sulphur yellow mushroom, with a strongly unpleasant smell reminiscent of coal-gas. The cap has either a convex or swollen centre and is smooth and dry.

**Group** Mushrooms and Toadstools.
**Season** Autumn.
**Edibility** Distinctly unpleasant.
**Cap** 4–8cm (1$^1$/2–3in) diameter.
**Stem** Cylindrical, smooth.
**Flesh** Firm, yellow.
**Spore deposit** White.
**Habitat** Solitary in deciduous woods, especially clay soils.

## TRICHOLOMA TERREUM  GREY TRICHOLOMA

A coniferous-wood species, having a dark grey, fibrous-scaly cap and white gills. Avoid eating all grey *Tricholoma* species. The cap is convex with a raised centre and sometimes splits to reveal the underlying white flesh.

**Group** Mushrooms and Toadstools.
**Season** Autumn.
**Edibility** Inedible.
**Cap** 3–8cm (1$^1$/4–3in) diameter.
**Stem** Cylindrical, white to greyish.
**Flesh** White or pale grey.
**Spore deposit** White.
**Habitat** Common in needle litter.

## COLLYBIA CONFLUENS CLUSTERED TOUGH SHANK

Greyish brown fruitbodies with tall, velvety stems, growing in dense tufts with stem bases fused. The cap is convex or flattened and smooth.

**Group** Mushrooms and Toadstools.
**Season** Autumn.
**Edibility** Worthless.
**Cap** 2–4cm ($^3/_4$–1$^1/_2$in) diameter.
**Stem** Tall, often flattened, with a layer of fine dense hairs.
**Flesh** Thin, pale, odourless.
**Spore deposit** Pale cream.
**Habitat** Amongst dead, fallen leaves.

## COLLYBIA MACULATA SPOTTED TOUGH SHANK

A common species which can be readily recognised by the reddish brown spotting of the white cap, stem and gills, and the very crowded, narrow gills.

**Group** Mushrooms and Toadstools.
**Season** Autumn.
**Edibility** Inedible, bitter and tough.
**Cap** 4–10cm (1$^1/_2$–4in) diameter.
**Stem** Tall, whitish, often spotted reddish brown.
**Flesh** White, firm with no smell.
**Spore deposit** Cream to pale pinkish.
**Habitat** Coniferous and deciduous woodland.

## COLLYBIA PERONATA WOOD WOOLLY FOOT

A thin-fleshed, yellowish brown mushroom, with a conspicuously hairy base to the stem. Often found attached to dead leaves.

**Group** Mushrooms and Toadstools.
**Season** Autumn.
**Edibility** Not recommended but can be dried for use as a condiment.
**Cap** 2–5cm (³/4–2in) diameter.
**Stem** Slender, yellowish, with a woolly-hairy base.
**Flesh** White or pale grey.
**Spore deposit** White.
**Habitat** All kinds of woodland.

## MYCENA PURA LILAC MYCENA

One of the larger Mycena species, distinguished by the pink to lilac colour, lack of a dark edge to the gills, and a smell that reminds one of radishes.

**Group** Mushrooms and Toadstools.
**Season** Autumn.
**Edibility** Poisonous.
**Cap** 2–6cm (³/4–2¹/4in) diameter.
**Stem** Slender but rigid, thicker towards the base.
**Flesh** Thin, pinkish with a radish smell.
**Spore deposit** White.
**Habitat** Among leaf-litter in deciduous woodland, especially under beech.

## AMANITA CITRINA  FALSE DEATH CAP

Recognised by the combination of a lemon-yellow or whitish cap with white scales, white gills, and a stem with a ring and a very swollen, rimmed base.

**Group** Mushrooms and Toadstools.
**Season** Summer and autumn.
**Edibility** <u>Avoid due to possible confusion with the Death Cap.</u>
**Cap** 4–8cm (1$^1$/2–3in) diameter.
**Stem** White, swollen at the base.
**Flesh** White, thick, smelling of raw potatoes.
**Spore deposit** White.
**Habitat** Solitary in pine and oak woods.

## AMANITA MUSCARIA  FLY AGARIC

Perhaps the best-known wild mushroom, having a large, scarlet cap with small white scales, and a membranous ring on the stem.

**Group** Mushrooms and Toadstools.
**Season** Autumn.
**Edibility** <u>Poisonous, can cause delirium and comas.</u>
**Cap** 2–9in (5–25cm) diameter.
**Stem** White, swollen at the base.
**Flesh** Thick, white.
**Spore deposit** White.
**Habitat** Groups under pine or birch.

## AMANITA PANTHERINA  THE PANTHER

An uncommon species, recognised by the brown cap with white scales, a flesh which does not redden on bruising, a striated cap margin, and a ring low on the stem.

**Group** Mushrooms and Toadstools.
**Season** Autumn.
**Edibility** <u>Very poisonous, deadly</u>.
**Cap** 5–10cm (2–4in) diameter.
**Stem** White, swollen at the base.
**Flesh** White, thick, smelling of raw potatoes.
**Spore deposit** White.
**Habitat** Solitary in pine or oak woods.

## AMANITA PHALLOIDES  DEATH CAP

Deadly poisonous, even in small amounts, always wash your hands after picking. Note the streaky, olive yellow cap, white gills, ring and sac-like volva on the stem.

**Group** Mushrooms and Toadstools.
**Season** Autumn.
**Edibility** <u>Deadly poisonous.</u>
**Cap** 6–12cm ($2^{1}/4$–$4^{3}/4$in) diameter.
**Stem** White, with a zigzag pattern.
**Flesh** White, with a sickly smell.
**Spore deposit** White.
**Habitat** Solitary in woodland, especially under oak trees.

## AMANITA RUBESCENS  THE BLUSHER

A very common, stocky *Amanita* species having a reddish brown cap with small greyish scales, and a flesh which turns pinkish on exposure.

**Group** Mushrooms and Toadstools.
**Season** Summer and autumn.
**Edibility** Only after cooking, avoid confusion with *A. pantherina*.
**Cap** 5–15cm (2–6in) diameter.
**Stem** Stocky, with a swollen base.
**Flesh** Thick, firm, white.
**Spore deposit** White.
**Habitat** Common in woods.

## CLITOPILUS PRUNULUS  THE MILLER

A whitish species, with decurrent gills, and a strong smell and taste of bread dough.

**Group** Mushrooms and Toadstools.
**Season** Summer and autumn.
**Edibility** Excellent.
**Cap** 3–10cm (1¼–4in) diameter.
**Stem** Short, white, smooth and solid.
**Flesh** Thick, white, with a strong smell.
**Spore deposit** Salmon-pink.
**Habitat** Forms small groups on ground or grassy glades.

## LEPIOTA CRISTATA  STINKING PARASOL

The small white caps have concentric rings of dark reddish brown scales, the gills are white, and there is a ring on the stem.

**Group** Mushrooms and Toadstools.
**Season** Autumn.
**Edibility** Inedible and possibly poisonous.
**Cap** 2–4cm (³/4–1¹/2in) diameter.
**Stem** Slender, white, hollow and smooth.
**Flesh** Thin, white, with a rubbery smell.
**Spore deposit** White.
**Habitat** Forms small troops among leaf-litter or short grass at edges of woods.

## LEPIOTA CASTANEA  CHESTNUT PARASOL

A small *Lepiota* species, with a brown, scaly cap and stem, and occurring in deciduous woodland.

**Group** Mushrooms and Toadstools.
**Season** Autumn.
**Edibility** Poisonous.
**Cap** 2–4cm (³/4–1¹/2in) diameter.
**Stem** Cylindrical, finely scaled.
**Flesh** Thin, pale yellowish with a fruity smell.
**Spore deposit** White.
**Habitat** Isolated or in small groups among leaf-litter.

## MACROLEPIOTA PROCERA PARASOL MUSHROOM

A large mushroom, with a woolly, scaly cap and a tall, scaly stem with a large, movable ring. There are young unexpanded fruitbodies resembling drum-sticks.

**Group** Mushrooms and Toadstools.
**Season** Summer and autumn.
**Edibility** One of the best edible species.
**Cap** 8–20cm (3–8in) diameter.
**Stem** Cylindrical with a snake-skin pattern.
**Flesh** Thick, white.
**Spore deposit** White.
**Habitat** In groups often forming fairy rings in woodland or meadows.

## AGARICUS AUGUSTUS THE PRINCE

One of the largest of the true mushrooms, with a yellowish brown, scaly cap, bruising deep yellow when rubbed.

**Group** Mushrooms and Toadstools.
**Season** Summer and autumn.
**Edibility** Excellent.
**Cap** 10–20cm (4–8in) diameter.
**Stem** Hollow, white, soft-scaly below ring.
**Flesh** White with a smell of almonds.
**Spore deposit** Brownish black.
**Habitat** On forest floor, under spruce or deciduous trees.

## STROPHARIA AERUGINOSA VERDIGRIS AGARIC

A common and distinctive toadstool having, a slimy, blue-green cap with white scales when young and fresh.

**Group** Mushrooms and Toadstools.
**Season** Autumn.
**Edibility** <u>Poisonous.</u>
**Cap** 3–8cm (1¼–3in) diameter.
**Stem** Cylindrical, hollow, slimy, white or pale green.
**Flesh** Whitish with a green tint.
**Spore deposit** Purplish brown.
**Habitat** In mixed woodland.

---

## HEBELOMA CRUSTULINIFORME FAIRY CAKE HEBELOMA

A common, clay-brown species which has a strong smell of radish and exudes droplets from the gills in damp weather.

**Group** Mushrooms and Toadstools.
**Season** Autumn.
**Edibility** <u>Poisonous, with a bitter taste.</u>
**Cap** 4–8cm (1½–3in) diameter.
**Stem** Cylindrical, white, powdery at the apex.
**Flesh** Thick, white with a radish smell.
**Spore deposit** Rusty brown.
**Habitat** In deciduous woodland.

## HEBELOMA SINAPIZANS CLAYEY HEBELOMA

This is the largest of the *Hebeloma* species, with a distinctive smell of raw potatoes.

**Group** Mushrooms and Toadstools.
**Season** Autumn.
**Edibility** Poisonous, causing upset stomachs.
**Cap** 7–15cm (2³/4–6in) diameter.
**Stem** Cylindrical, hollow, white with small scales.
**Flesh** White, thick.
**Spore deposit** Clay-brown.
**Habitat** In leaf-litter in deciduous woods.

## INOCYBE FASTIGIATA PEAKED INOCYBE

A very common, large *Inocybe* species, with a conical, yellowish brown cap, and a smell of mouldy bread.

**Group** Mushrooms and Toadstools.
**Season** Summer and autumn.
**Edibility** Causes muscarine poisoning and must be avoided.
**Cap** 5–7cm (2–2³/4in) diameter.
**Stem** Cylindrical, hollow, white to ochre-brown, fibrous.
**Flesh** Pale, firm with a distinctive smell.
**Spore deposit** Pale clay-brown.
**Habitat** Always under trees, often beech.

## CORTINARIUS SPECIOSISSIMUS   FOXY ORANGE CORTINARIUS

A fairly rare species, with pointed tawny brown cap, growing in coniferous woods.

**Group** Mushrooms and Toadstools.
**Season** Autumn.
**Edibility** Deadly poisonous, attacking the liver.
**Cap** 3–8cm (1¼–3in) diameter.
**Stem** Ochre to tawny brown, slightly thickened towards the base.
**Flesh** Yellowish with a faint smell of radish.
**Spore deposit** Cinnamon brown.
**Habitat** Uncommon, among mosses.

## LACTARIUS TORMINOSUS   WOOLLY MILK-CAP

The shaggy, zoned cap with a strongly inrolled margin distinguishes this birch-wood species.

**Group** Mushrooms and Toadstools.
**Season** Autumn.
**Edibility** Poisonous.
**Cap** 5–15cm (2–6in) diameter.
**Stem** Smooth, dry, pinkish.
**Flesh** White to pink, with a white latex.
**Spore deposit** Pale pinkish cream.
**Habitat** Always with birch, in damp areas.

## RUSSULA XERAMPELINA  CRAB RUSSULA

An extremely variable species, but easily recognised by the strong smell of crab.

**Group** Mushrooms and Toadstools.
**Season** Autumn.
**Edibility** Good with a mild nutty taste.
**Cap** 5–15cm (2–6in) diameter.
**Stem** White, enlarged towards the base.
**Flesh** White with a mild taste.
**Spore deposit** Ochre.
**Habitat** Under beech or oak trees.

## RUSSULA EMETICA  EMETIC RUSSULA

A bright red *Russula* of coniferous woodland, with a very peppery flesh.

**Group** Mushrooms and Toadstools.
**Season** Autumn.
**Edibility** Inedible, causes vomiting if eaten raw.
**Cap** 3–6cm (1¹/₄–2¹/₄in) diameter.
**Stem** Pure white, brittle.
**Flesh** Thick, white with an acrid taste.
**Spore deposit** White.
**Habitat** Coniferous woodland.

## RUSSULA CYANOXANTHA  BLUE AND YELLOW RUSSULA

A common species of deciduous woods. Characterised by the variable cap colour, white gills and mild taste.

**Group** Mushrooms and Toadstools.
**Season** Autumn.
**Edibility** Good edible species.
**Cap** 5–15cm (2–6in) diameter.
**Stem** White, firm, cylindrical.
**Flesh** White with a mild taste.
**Spore deposit** White.
**Habitat** In deciduous woods.

---

## PAXILLUS INVOLUTUS  BROWN ROLL-RIM

A very common, large species with a short stem, and brown gills which feel slimy when squashed.

**Group** Boletes.
**Season** Summer and autumn.
**Edibility** Poisonous, thought to have an accumulative toxin. To be avoided.
**Cap** 4–20cm (1¹/₂–8in) diameter.
**Stem** Yellowish, thick, soft.
**Flesh** White with a mild taste.
**Spore deposit** Clay-brown.
**Habitat** In mixed woods or heathland.

## BOLETUS EDULIS CEP OR PENNY BUN BOLETUS

A robust species recognised by the brown cap, pale stem with white network on the upper part, and white unchanging flesh.

**Group** Boletes.
**Season** Autumn.
**Edibility** Good edible species, used as a commercial flavouring in soups.
**Cap** 8–20cm (3–8in) diameter.
**Stem** Whitish or pale brown.
**Flesh** Whitish.
**Spore deposit** Olive-brown.
**Habitat** All types of woodland, mostly beech and oak.

## BOLETUS SATANAS DEVIL'S BOLETUS

A large distinctive species having a whitish cap, red pores and a distinct red network on the stem.

**Group** Boletes.
**Season** Summer.
**Edibility** Poisonous.
**Cap** 8–25cm (3–9in) diameter.
**Stem** Short, stout, covered with red network of raised lines.
**Flesh** Pale straw or whitish and unpleasant smell.
**Spore deposit** Olive-brown.
**Habitat** In woods, usually with conifers.

## LECCINUM SCABRUM BROWN BIRCH BOLETE

A very common species, belonging to a group sometimes known as the 'rough shanks' owing to their scaly stems.

**Group** Boletes.
**Season** Summer and autumn.
**Edibility** Excellent.
**Cap** 4–10cm (1½–4in) diameter.
**Stem** Off-white with tiny, black scales.
**Flesh** Thick, soft, white.
**Spore deposit** Cinnamon-brown.
**Habitat** On the ground, under birch trees.

## LECCINUM VERSIPELLE ORANGE BIRCH BOLETE

Commonly found in birch woods, this species is characterised by a distinctly orange cap and a blackening flesh.

**Group** Boletes.
**Season** Summer and autumn.
**Edibility** Good.
**Cap** 8–15cm (3–6in) diameter.
**Stem** Tall, white with small, black scales.
**Flesh** Thick, white, discolouring black when exposed to air.
**Spore deposit** Cinnamon-brown.
**Habitat** Numerous in birch woods.

## GYROMITRA ESCULENTA  TURBAN FUNGUS

A conifer-wood species having a much-lobed, brain-like reddish brown cap and a short, whitish stalk.

**Group** Cup Fungi.
**Season** Spring.
**Edibility** <u>Poisonous; deadly if eaten raw, can be harmful even after cooking</u>.
**Cap** 3–9cm (1¼–3½in) diameter.
**Stem** Whitish, either grooved, smooth or slightly scurfy.
**Flesh** Thin, whitish, brittle.
**Habitat** With conifers, especially pines, growing on sandy soil.

---

## HELVELLA ACETABULUM  RIBBED-STALK CUP

A common species having a whitish, saddle-shaped cap and deeply furrowed, whitish stalk.

**Group** Cup Fungi.
**Season** Spring.
**Edibility** <u>Poisonous.</u>
**Cap** 3–7cm (1¼–2¾in) diameter.
**Stem** Whitish, furrowed vertical grooves.
**Flesh** Thin, brittle, white.
**Habitat** In deciduous or mixed woodland, often at path edges.

## DISCIOTIS VENOSA  VEINED CUP

A large, brown, thick-fleshed, saucer-shaped species, with a strongly veined upper surface, and a very short, stout stem.

**Group** Cup Fungi.
**Season** Spring.
**Edibility** Poisonous.
**Fruitbody** Up to18cm (7in) across.
**Stem** Very short, stout, often sunk in the soil.
**Flesh** Thick, brittle. Pale brownish, with an unpleasant smell.
**Habitat** On soil in woods and in grass.

## PEZIZA BADIA  PIG'S EARS

A cup-or saucer-shaped species having fruitbodies with dark olive-brown inner surfaces and red-brown outer surfaces. Lacks any stalk.

**Group** Cup Fungi.
**Season** Summer and autumn.
**Edibility** Poisonous when eaten raw, must be well cooked.
**Fruitbody** 3–10cm (1¹/4–4in) diameter.
**Flesh** Thin, reddish brown, brittle.
**Habitat** Found on bare, sandy soil, often growing in clusters.

## CAMAROPHYLLUS PRATENSIS BUFF MEADOW CAP

A fleshy, orange-buff wax cup, which is regarded as a good, edible species.

**Group** Mushrooms and Toadstools.
**Season** Autumn.
**Edibility** Excellent.
**Cap** 3–9cm (1¼–3½in) across.
**Stem** Cylindrical or tapering at the base.
**Flesh** Thick, white and firm.
**Spore deposit** White.
**Habitat** In open grassland.

## HYGROCYBE CONICA CONICAL WAX CAP

The most common of the brightly coloured wax caps which blacken at maturity. The cap is conical, pointed and bright orange in colour.

**Group** Mushrooms and Toadstools.
**Season** Summer and autumn.
**Edibility** Inedible, to be avoided.
**Cap** 2–5cm (¾–2in) across.
**Stem** Cylindrical, fibrous and splitting easily, yellowish.
**Flesh** Thin, watery, pale.
**Spore deposit** White.
**Habitat** Commonly found anywhere among grass.

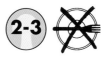

## HYGROCYBE COCCINEA SCARLET HOOD

A grassland species, distinguished by the bright red cap, gills and stem.

**Group** Mushrooms and Toadstools.
**Season** Summer and autumn.
**Edibility** Edible.
**Size cap** 3–5cm (1¼–2in) across.
**Stem** Cylindrical, scarlet-red, paler at the base, hollow, smooth.
**Flesh** Thin, yellow, watery.
**Spore deposit** White.
**Habitat** In grassland.

---

## CALOCYBE GAMBOSA  ST GEORGE'S MUSHROOM

This large, whitish mushroom is usually much sought after as it is one of the few good edible species to occur in spring. Prefers a chalky soil.

**Group** Mushrooms and Toadstools.
**Season** Spring.
**Edibility** Good.
**Cap** 5–10cm (2–4in) across.
**Stem** Short, stocky, solid, white and smooth.
**Flesh** Thick, white and firm.
**Spore deposit** White.
**Habitat** Among grass.

## CLITOCYBE RIVULOSA CRACKING CLITOCYBE

Forms fairy rings on lawns and may be found mixed with the Fairy Ring Champignon *Marasmius oreades*.

**Group** Mushrooms and Toadstools.
**Season** Autumn.
**Edibility** <u>Poisonous, causing muscarine poisoning.</u>
**Cap** 2–5cm (³/4–2in) across.
**Stem** Short cylindrical.
**Flesh** White and soft.
**Spore deposit** White.
**Habitat** In troops in short grass.

## MARASMIUS OREADES FAIRY RING CHAMPIGNON

An unpopular species with gardeners owing to its habit of forming extensive fairy rings which last for many years.

**Group** Mushrooms and Toadstools.
**Season** Summer and autumn.
**Edibility** Edible and good, used in stews.
**Cap** 2–5cm (³/4–2in) across.
**Stem** Thin, tough, dry.
**Flesh** Thin, white with a smell of hay.
**Spore deposit** White.
**Habitat** Large numbers in grassland, especially lawns.

## ENTOLOMA RHODOPOLIUM ROSY ENTOLOMA

This is a tall but fragile mushroom, distinguished by the pinkish gills and an odour of flour. As it is poisonous, all pink-gilled mushrooms are best avoided.

**Group** Mushrooms and Toadstools.
**Season** Summer.
**Edibility** Poisonous, causing stomach upsets.
**Cap** 2–10cm (3/4–4in) across.
**Stem** Cylindrical, white, smooth.
**Flesh** Thick, brittle.
**Spore deposit** Pink.
**Habitat** Small groups among leaf-litter in deciduous woods.

## LEUCOAGARICUS NAUCINUS SMOOTH LEPIOTA

A fleshy grassland fungus, differing from the true mushrooms in having gills which remain white.

**Group** Mushrooms and Toadstools.
**Season** Summer and autumn.
**Edibility** Poisonous, causing stomach upsets.
**Cap** 5–10cm (2–4in) across.
**Stem** Short and stocky, smooth, white.
**Flesh** Thin, soft, yellowish.
**Spore deposit** White.
**Habitat** Among grass, especially on lawns.

ON THE GROUND IN GRASSLANDS

## LEUCOCOPRINUS CEPAESTIPES ONION-STALKED LEPIOTA

A white, tufted mushroom, it is recognised by the swollen stem base. Found during the summer months in warmer regions, it often occurs in hot-houses all year round.

**Group** Mushrooms and Toadstools.
**Season** Summer.
**Edibility** Possibly poisonous, inedible.
**Cap** 3–7cm (1¹/₄–2³/₄in) across.
**Stem** Slender with a swollen base.
**Flesh** Thin, white and soft.
**Spore deposit** White.
**Habitat** Among grass or leaf-litter.

## LEUCOCOPRINUS LUTEUS YELLOW COTTONY AGARIC

The fruitbody is uniformly sulphur-yellow, with a powdery cap, and grows in tufts. The fungus often occurs in hot houses all year round and in warmer regions during the summer months.

**Group** Mushrooms and Toadstools.
**Season** Summer.
**Edibility** Possibly poisonous, inedible.
**Cap** 3–5cm (1¹/₄–2in) across.
**Stem** Slender, sulphur-yellow, smooth.
**Flesh** Thin, soft and yellowish.
**Spore deposit** White.
**Habitat** Among grass, on bare soil or among leaf-litter.

## MACROLEPIOTA EXCORIATA FLAKY LEPIOTA

A large, fleshy mushroom with white gills, sometimes found growing in large troops in meadows.

**Group** Mushrooms and Toadstools.
**Season** Summer and autumn.
**Edibility** Good.
**Cap** 4–8cm (1 1/2–3in) across.
**Stem** Cylindrical, white, smooth.
**Flesh** Thick, soft and white.
**Spore deposit** White.
**Habitat** Among grass, often on cultivated land.

## MACROLEPIOTA GRACILENTA SLENDER LEPIOTA

One of the tall Macrolepiota species, characterised by the small, tawny brown scales.

**Group** Mushrooms and Toadstools.
**Season** Summer and autumn.
**Edibility** Good.
**Cap** 7–15cm (2 3/4–6in) across.
**Stem** Tall, cylindrical with a swollen base.
**Flesh** Thick, white and soft.
**Spore deposit** White.
**Habitat** Forming troops on pastureland.

## CHLOROPHYLLUM MOLYBDITES GREEN-SPORED LEPIOTA

A large, white fleshy mushroom found on lawns. Frequently confused with the parasol mushrooms but differs with the green gills.

**Group** Mushrooms and Toadstools.
**Season** Summer.
**Edibility** <u>Possibly poisonous, can cause serious stomach upsets and vomiting.</u>
**Cap** 5–15cm (2–6in) across.
**Stem** Cylindrical, brownish, fibrous.
**Flesh** Pale pinkish, thick.
**Spore deposit** Pea-green.
**Habitat** Among grass, lawns; not present in Europe.

## AGARICUS ARVENSIS HORSE MUSHROOM

A common, grassland true mushroom, which discolours yellowish on bruising. Take care when eating species which bruise yellow.

**Group** Mushrooms and Toadstools.
**Season** Autumn.
**Edibility** Good.
**Cap** 7–15cm (2³/₄–6in) across.
**Stem** Cylindrical, smooth, white.
**Flesh** Thick, white, aroma of almonds.
**Spore deposit** Blackish-brown.
**Habitat** Common on pastureland.

## AGARICUS CAMPESTRIS FIELD MUSHROOM

The best-known mushroom, commonly illustrated in biology textbooks, distinguished by the reddening flesh, and the small, simple ring on the stem.

**Group** Mushrooms and Toadstools.
**Season** Summer and autumn.
**Edibility** Good.
**Cap** 3–8cm (1¹/₄–3in) across.
**Stem** Short, cylindrical, white, smooth.
**Flesh** Thick and white.
**Spore deposit** Blackish-brown.
**Habitat** Common in open grassland.

## AGARICUS XANTHODERMUS YELLOW-STAINING MUSHROOM

A large and common, true mushroom, which bruises yellow, and is recognisable by the bright yellow discolouration of the flesh at the stem base.

**Group** Mushrooms and Toadstools.
**Season** Summer and autumn.
**Edibility** Poisonous, causing severe stomach upsets and even coma.
**Cap** 6–12cm (1¹/₄–4³/₄in) across.
**Stem** Cylindrical, white, smooth.
**Flesh** Soft, white, carbolic odour.
**Spore deposit** Purplish-brown.
**Habitat** Under hedges or besides paths.

## PANAEOLINA FOENISECII  BROWN HAY CAP

A very common toadstool found on many lawns from summer onwards. They have distinctive mottled gills and a zoned cap.

**Group** Mushrooms and Toadstools.
**Season** Summer and autumn.
**Edibility** Inedible, mildly hallucinogenic in children.
**Cap** 1–2cm ($^3/8$–$^3/4$in) diameter.
**Stem** Short, cylindrical, smooth.
**Flesh** Thin, whitish.
**Spore deposit** Blackish brown.
**Habitat** Ubiquitous on lawns.

## CONOCYBE FILARIS  THREAD CONE CAP

A small, slender cone cap, characterised by a membranous ring on the stem.

**Group** Mushrooms and Toadstools.
**Season** Summer and autumn.
**Edibility** Deadly poisonous.
**Cap** 0.5–1cm ($^3/16$–$^3/8$in) diameter.
**Stem** Cylindrical, cream-coloured.
**Flesh** Thin, brown.
**Spore deposit** Rusty brown.
**Habitat** On clay soil, often in pastures.

## PSILOCYBE SEMILANCEATA LIBERTY CAP

A well-known species, owing to its reputation as a 'magic mushroom'.

**Group** Mushrooms and Toadstools.
**Season** Autumn.
**Edibility** <u>Toxic causing psychotropic poisoning, used as a hallucinogen.</u>
**Cap** 1–1.5cm ($^3/_8$–$^5/_8$in) diameter.
**Stem** Slender, cylindrical.
**Flesh** Thin, firm.
**Spore deposit** Purplish black.
**Habitat** Very common in open grassland, either solitary or in large groups.

## STROPHARIA CORONILLA GARLAND STROPHARIA

A pale yellow mushroom, easily mistaken for the true mushroom.

**Group** Mushrooms and Toadstools.
**Season** Summer and autumn.
**Edibility** <u>Believed to be poisonous.</u>
**Cap** 2–6cm ($^3/4$–$2^1/4$in) diameter.
**Stem** Short, cylindrical, white.
**Flesh** Thick, white and soft.
**Spore deposit** Dark purplish brown.
**Habitat** In groups among short grass, including lawns.

## INOCYBE PATOUILLARDII RED INOCYBE

One of the large species of *Inocybe*, distinguished by the red staining on handling; often found in the springtime.

**Group** Mushrooms and Toadstools.
**Season** Summer and autumn.
**Edibility** <u>Poisonous, can be deadly, causing muscarine poisoning.</u>
**Cap** 3–7cm (1$^1$/4–2$^3$/4in) diameter.
**Stem** Cylindrical, white, smooth, robust.
**Flesh** White becoming reddish when broken open.
**Spore deposit** Cinnamon-brown.
**Habitat** In groups in pastureland, often associated with beech trees.

---

## LANGERMANNIA GIGANTEA GIANT PUFFBALL

Probably the easiest of all fungi to recognise, forming large ball-shaped structures up to 160cm (63in) in diameter.

**Group** Puffballs and allies.
**Season** Summer.
**Edibility** Edible and delicious.
**Fruitbody** 15–60cm (6–24in) diameter.
**Flesh** White, becoming brown with age, firm.
**Spore deposit** Brown.
**Habitat** Singly or in groups, can form large fairy rings.

# MORCHELLA ESCULENTA COMMON MOREL

A robust, club-shaped species recognised by the pale brownish, honeycomb-like head and white, scurfy stem.

**Group** Cup-fungi.
**Season** Spring.
**Edibility** Never eat raw. Edible.
**Cap** 5–10cm (2–4in) diameter.
**Stem** Swollen at the base, irregularly ribbed and furrowed, white, hollow.
**Flesh** Brittle, thin, whitish.
**Spore deposit** Ochraceous.
**Habitat** Open scrub, chalky soil, in dune slacks.

---

# MORCHELLA SEMILIBERA HALF FREE MOREL

A distinctive, spring-fruiting species recognised by the pendant, conical, honey-combed cap, the lower half of which is free from the stem.

**Group** Cup-fungi.
**Season** Spring.
**Edibility** Edible but should always be cooked.
**Cap** 1.5–4cm ($^5/8$–$2^1/2$in) diameter.
**Stem** Hollow, whitish, often tall.
**Flesh** Thin, brittle, whitish.
**Habitat** Damp soil in woods, in hedges or on waste ground.

## PLEUROTUS OSTREATUS  OYSTER MUSHROOM

A well-known edible species, growing in tiers on trunks and stumps of frondose trees, with a greyish brown cap and lateral attachment.

**Group** Bracket-fungi.
**Season** Summer, autumn and winter.
**Edibility** Excellent, grown commercially.
**Cap** 3–7cm (1$^1$/4–2$^3$/4in) diameter.
**Stem** None, or very short.
**Flesh** Thick, white.
**Spore deposit** Very pale lilac.
**Habitat** On stumps and trunks of frondose trees, especially beech.

## FLAMMULINA VELUTIPES  VELVET SHANK

A tufted mushroom, growing on trees during the winter months, recognised by the velvety stem and slimy cap.

**Group** Mushrooms and Toadstools.
**Season** Autumn, winter, spring.
**Edibility** Edible.
**Cap** 3–6cm (1$^1$/4–2$^1$/4in) diameter.
**Stem** Tough, finely velvety, yellowish above becoming blackish brown below.
**Flesh** Soft, white.
**Spore deposit** White.
**Habitat** Tufted on deciduous trees, especially elm.

## GALERINA UNICOLOUR MARGINATE GALERINA

A common species recognised by the brown colours, clustered habit, stem with ring, and slightly striate cap margins.

**Group** Mushrooms and Toadstools.
**Season** Autumn.
**Edibility** Deadly poisonous.
**Cap** 2–5cm (³/4–2in) diameter.
**Stem** Surface bears whitish fibrils.
**Flesh** Pale brown.
**Spore deposit** Brown.
**Habitat** Clustered on dead wood and twigs, especially in coniferous woods.

## PHOLIOTA SQUARROSA SHAGGY PHOLIOTA

Forms large, dense clusters at the base of tree-trunks, with yellowish brown caps and stems covered with pointed scales.

**Group** Mushrooms and Toadstools.
**Season** Summer and autumn.
**Edibility** Poisonous.
**Cap** 6–10cm (2¹/4–4in) diameter.
**Stem** Cylindrical, fibrous, firm.
**Flesh** Thick, cream-coloured.
**Habitat** Dense tufts at the base of deciduous trees, especially ash.

## GYMNOPILUS JUNONIUS ORANGE PHOLIOTA

Often called *Pholiota spectabilis* in older books, this large golden-brown mushroom, with a ring on the stem, forms small clusters at the base of tree-trunks.

**Group** Mushrooms and Toadstools.
**Season** Autumn.
**Edibility** Poisonous.
**Cap** 6–12cm (2$\frac{1}{4}$–4$\frac{3}{4}$in) diameter.
**Stem** Cylindrical, robust.
**Flesh** Thick, yellowish.
**Spore deposit** Rusty brown.
**Habitat** Dense tufts at base of tree trunks, especially ash and apple.

## GYMNOPILUS PENETRANS FRECKLE-GILLED GYMNOPILUS

A very common toadstool, found in large numbers in conifer woods in the autumn, with a tawny brown cap and rusty brown, spotted gills.

**Group** Mushrooms and Toadstools.
**Season** Autumn.
**Edibility** Inedible, with a bitter taste.
**Cap** 3–6cm (1$\frac{1}{4}$–2$\frac{1}{4}$in) diameter.
**Flesh** Thin, yellowish.
**Spore deposit** Rusty brown.
**Habitat** Common in coniferous woods.

## TUBARIA FURFURACEA  MEALY TUBARIA

A very common toadstool, growing on woody debris, and recognised primarily by the brown, decurrent gills, and the white flecks on the cap.

**Group** Mushrooms and Toadstools.
**Season** Throughout the year.
**Edibility** Inedible.
**Cap** 2–4cm ($^3$/4–1$^1$/2in) diameter.
**Stem** Woolly based.
**Flesh** Thin, brown.
**Spore deposit** Yellowish brown.
**Habitat** Found in large numbers on debris from deciduous trees.

---

## CREPIDOTUS MOLLIS  SOFT SLIPPER TOADSTOOL

One of the larger slipper toadstools, recognised in the field by an elastic layer which is observed when the cap is pulled apart.

**Group** Mushrooms and Toadstools.
**Season** Summer and autumn.
**Edibility** Inedible.
**Cap** 2–7cm ($^3$/4–2$^3$/4in) diameter.
**Stem** None.
**Flesh** Thin, white with a gelatinised layer.
**Spore deposit** Snuff-brown.
**Habitat** Found on dead and rotting branches, often in large numbers.

## CORIOLUS VERSICOLOUR VARICOLOURED BRACKET

An extremely common bracket-fungus, forming clusters and overlapping tiers on dead wood.

**Group** Bracket-fungi.
**Season** Throughout the year.
**Edibility** Inedible.
**Cap** 3–8cm (1$^1$/4–3in) diameter.
**Tubes** Shallow, white.
**Flesh** White and tough.
**Spore deposit** White.
**Habitat** Groups on dead deciduous trees and stumps.

## TYROMYCES LACTEUS MILK-WHITE POLYPORE

A soft, white bracket, commonly found on deciduous trees.

**Group** Bracket-fungi.
**Season** Summer and autumn.
**Edibility** Inedible.
**Cap** 2–6cm ($^3$/4–2$^1$/4in) diameter.
**Tubes** White.
**Flesh** Thick, soft, white, fibrous.
**Spore deposit** White.
**Habitat** On deciduous trees.

## GANODERMA LUCIDUM SHINING GANODERMA

A stalked species of *Ganoderma*, easily recognised by the strong varnished crust of the cap and stem.

**Group** Bracket-fungi.
**Season** Throughout the year.
**Edibility** Inedible.
**Cap** 3–30cm (1$^1$/4–12in) diameter.
**Tubes** Brown.
**Flesh** Pale brown, corky.
**Spore deposit** Cinnamon-brown.
**Habitat** On roots of oak, also other deciduous trees.

---

## MERULIUS TREMELLOSUS JELLY ROT

Small gelatinous brackets, with a pinkish orange, wrinkled lower surface, found growing on dead wood. The fruitbody spreads over the wood and curves at the upper margin to form small brackets.

**Group** Bracket-fungi.
**Season** Autumn.
**Edibility** Inedible.
**Fruitbody** 2–4cm ($^3$/4–1$^1$/2in) diameter.
**Flesh** Thin, soft and gelatinous.
**Spore deposit** White.
**Habitat** On rotting wood, especially found on the underside of fallen trunks.

ON TREES, STUMPS AND DEBRIS

## STEREUM HIRSUTUM YELLOW STEREUM

The most common *Stereum* species, forming many yellowish brackets growing in tiers on dead branches.

**Group** Bracket-fungi.
**Season** Throughout the year.
**Edibility** Inedible.
**Cap** 2–6cm ($^3$/4–2$^1$/4in) diameter.
**Flesh** Thick, yellowish, leathery-tough.
**Spore deposit** White.
**Habitat** On dead wood of deciduous trees, especially oak, beech and alder.

## LYCOPERDON PYRIFORME STUMP PUFFBALL

A common species distinguished by the clustered, pear-shaped fruitbodies which grow on wood and have white, cord-like mycelium at the base.

**Group** Puffballs.
**Season** Summer and autumn.
**Edibility** Edible when young and white inside.
**Fruitbody** 4–8cm (1$^1$/2–3in) diameter.
**Sterile base** Spongy.
**Fertile tissue** White turning finally to olive-brown.
**Habitat** On clusters on old stumps and logs or attached to buried wood.

## CALOCERA VISCOSA JELLY ANTLER FUNGUS

A common species recognised by the branched, orange-yellow, tough gelatinous fruitbodies which grow on conifer stumps.

**Group** Jelly Fungi.
**Season** Autumn and winter.
**Edibility** Inedible.
**Fruitbody** 2–8cm ($^3/_4$–3in) diameter.
**Flesh** Tough, gelatinous, yellow.
**Spore deposit** Yellow.
**Habitat** On old stumps of coniferous trees, especially pines.

## TREMELLA MESENTERICA YELLOW BRAIN FUNGUS

A distinctive species recognised by the orange-yellow colour, gelatinous flesh and irregular, brain-like shape.

**Group** Jelly Fungi.
**Season** Autumn and winter.
**Edibility** Inedible.
**Fruitbody** 1–8cm ($^3/_8$–3in) diameter.
**Flesh** Thick, soft, white, fibrous.
**Spore deposit** White.
**Habitat** On dead branches of deciduous trees; common.

## BULGARIA INQUINANS BLACK BULGAR

A common species, which is recognised by the blackish, thick-fleshed, rubbery, clustered fruitbodies.

**Group** Cup Fungi.
**Season** Autumn.
**Edibility** Inedible.
**Cap** 1–4cm ($^3/8$–1$^1/2$in) diameter.
**Flesh** Thick, gelatinous, blackish.
**Spore deposit** Blackish.
**Habitat** Clustered on dead trunks of deciduous trees, especially oak.

## HYPOXYLON MULTIFORME BIRCH CUSHION

A common species recognised by the red-brown then blackish, distinctly papillate fruitbodies which grow on birch and alder. The fruitbody is cushion-shaped or irregular, often developing an extensive crust.

**Group** Flask Fungi.
**Season** Summer and autumn.
**Edibility** Inedible.
**Cap** 1–3cm ($^1/2$–1$^1/4$in) diameter.
**Flesh** Thick, black, brittle.
**Spore deposit** Black.
**Habitat** On dead branches of birch and alder.

## HYPHOLOMA ELONGATUM SWAMP SULPHUR CAP

Commonly found in large groups among *Sphagnum* moss, and recognised by the yellowish cap and stem.

**Group** Mushrooms and Toadstools.
**Season** Summer and autumn.
**Edibility** Inedible.
**Cap** 1–3cm ($^3$/8–1$^1$/4in) diameter.
**Stem** Tall, hollow, yellowish brown.
**Flesh** Thin, white, brittle.
**Spore deposit** Sooty brown.
**Habitat** Among *Sphagnum* moss, growing in marshland.

## NAUCORIA ESCHAROIDES CAMPANULATE NAUCORIA

Pale colours and occurrence in damp places under alders distinguish this common species.

**Group** Mushrooms and Toadstools.
**Season** Autumn.
**Edibility** Inedible.
**Cap** 0.8–2.5cm ($^5$/16–1in) diameter.
**Stem** Cylindrical, slender, smooth.
**Flesh** Thin, pale brown or yellowish.
**Spore deposit** Brown.
**Habitat** Gregarious, on damp ground under alders.

## PHOLIOTA HIGHLANDENSIS CHARCOAL PHOLIOTA

A very common toadstool on burnt ground and charred wood, distinguished by the slimy cap and reddish brown gills.

**Group** Mushrooms and Toadstools.
**Season** Autumn.
**Edibility** Inedible.
**Size cap** 3–5cm (1$^1$/4–2in) diameter.
**Stem** Short, yellowish brown.
**Flesh** Thin, pale, firm.
**Spore deposit** Cinnamon-brown.
**Habitat** On burnt ground or burnt stumps.

## RHIZINA UNDULATA PINE FIRE FUNGUS

Forms distinctive, dark brown, convex fruitbodies having a pale margin and firm flesh, and attached to the substrate by whitish root-like structures.

**Group** Cup Fungi.
**Season** Summer and autumn.
**Edibility** Inedible.
**Fruitbody** 4–12cm (1$^1$/2–4$^3$/4in) diameter.
**Flesh** Firm, tough, thick, reddish brown.
**Habitat** Usually on burnt ground in coniferous woods. Can cause a disease of conifers known as group dying.

# VOLVARIELLA SPECIOSA ROSE-GILLED GRISETTE

A tall, solitary, pale mushroom with a
sticky cap, pink gills, and a sac-like
volva.

**Group** Mushrooms and Toadstools.
**Season** Autumn.
**Edibility** Edible, but do not confuse with
the poisonous *Amanita* species.
**Cap** 7–14cm (2³/4–5¹/2in) diameter.
**Stem** Tall, fragile, cylindrical, whitish.
**Flesh** Thin, soft and soon decaying.
**Spore deposit** Salmon-pink.
**Habitat** Grows on compost heaps, and
richly manured soil.

# STROPHARIA SEMIGLOBATA DUNG ROUNDHEAD

A distinctive species recognised by the
yellowish, hemispherical, slimy cap, thin
ring on stem, and habit.

**Group** Mushrooms and Toadstools.
**Season** Summer and autumn.
**Edibility** Inedible.
**Cap** 1–4cm (³/8–1¹/2in) diameter.
**Stem** Cylindrical, whitish.
**Flesh** Pale, thin with no particular smell.
**Spore deposit** Purplish brown.
**Habitat** On dung of herbivores,
especially horse and cattle.

## NYCTALIS ASTEROPHORA POWDER CAP

A small toadstool having powdery caps
and growing in clusters on very rotten
fruitbodies of the Blackening Russula.

**Group** Mushrooms and Toadstools.
**Season** Autumn.
**Edibility** Worthless.
**Cap** 1–2cm ($^3$/8–$^3$/4in) diameter.
**Stem** Short, cylindrical, white.
**Flesh** Thin, white.
**Spore deposit** White.
**Habitat** Found on rotting fruitbodies of the
Blackening Russula (*Russula nigricans*).

## XEROCOMUS PARASITICUS PARASITIC BOLETE

The parasitic habit on the Common
Earthball (*Scleroderma citrinum*) is a
diagnostic character for this species.

**Group** Mushrooms and Toadstools.
**Season** Autumn.
**Edibility** Edible.
**Cap** 2–4cm ($^3$/4–1$^1$/2in) diameter.
**Stem** Cylindrical or tapered.
**Spore deposit** Brownish.
**Habitat** Parasitic on fruitbodies of the
Common Earthball.

# Index  Alphabetical listing of botanical names.

**I N D E X**

# Index Alphabetical listing of common names.

INDEX